Marketing Basics For Small Business Owners

Brought To You By
Jeff Visaya
www.JVVEnterprise.com

<u>Make No Promises, Tell No Lies! (Disclaimer)</u>

As much as I'd love to think that everyone who follows the advice in "Marketing Basics For Small Business Owners" will become fabulously wealthy by result, the truth is that I can't promise that will happen for you.

I can't guarantee that you will actually read the book, follow my suggestions to the letter and handle your business in professional manner that will make customers flock to your company.

I wish I could, but I can't. So here's the nitty gritty legal statement.

Legal Notices and Disclaimer

THE FOLLOWING TERMS AND CONDITIONS APPLY:
While all attempts have been made to verify information provided, neither myself, nor any ancillary party, assumes any responsibility for errors, omissions, or contradictory interpretation of the subject matter herein.

Any perceived slights of specific people or organizations are unintentional.

To the fullest extent permitted by applicable laws, in no event shall Marketing Basics For Small Business Owners, agents or suppliers be liable for damages of any kind or character, including without limitation any compensatory, incidental, direct, indirect, special, punitive, or consequential damages, loss of use, loss of data, loss of income or profit, loss of or damage to property, claims of third parties, or other losses of any kind or character, even if Marketing Basics has been advised of the possibility of such damages or losses, arising out of or in connection with the use of the Marketing Basics or any web site with which it is linked.

Table of Contents

__Introduction__

What is marketing? Most people have an idea what marketing is. It's trying to sell something to someone, right? Well, that's basically right. But there's a lot more to it than that. There's a lot of other stuff that you need to know.

And it's all that other stuff that is most important to you. Because it's all that *other stuff* that will make the difference between you being a success or a failure. It's the other stuff that will determine whether you barely make any money with your service or whether you become rich beyond your wildest dreams.

And that's what this book is all about. You are about to discover how to plan a successful marketing strategy. This book is about to tell you everything you'll ever need to know about marketing and how to take your own business to the next level and beyond.

So let's get started...

Chapter One

The Basics of Marketing

Before we get into what marketing is all about and how you can achieve success with your very own marketing plan, there's something that needs to be mentioned first.

That something is this:

Before you go ahead and start marketing yourself, make sure you're ready for a lot of business. Also, make sure you know what you're doing and that you're good at what you do.

To put it plainly:

> ➤ Make sure you have something that's truly ready to be marketed and make sure you're ready to back-up everything that you say through your marketing plan.

No matter what type of service you offer, you'd better know what you're doing. Furthermore, you'd better be ready to accept a lot of new customers. After all, you're launching a marketing campaign so that you can attract new customers. You don't want to be forced to turn customers away.

Even worse, you don't want to gather customers and then not be able to deliver a great service. You don't want be unable to perform your service well. You also don't want to have too little time to actually take care of all your customers.

You only get one shot at impressing customers. If you do a bad job then news of that will spread like a wild fire and then all your marketing efforts will never work again and your business will fail.

So make sure you're ready before you actually launch any marketing campaigns. Don't trick yourself into thinking you'll deal with future problems when they arise. And don't fool yourself into thinking that it would be a wonderful problem to have too many customers.

If your marketing efforts work (and they will if you follow what you're about to discover in this book) then you will have a lot of customers. However, if you don't treat those customers right, because of one thing or many things you do wrong, then your business will dry up. And then it won't matter how much or how well you market your business, you will never achieve any real level of success.

So, before you do anything else, make sure you and your business are ready to handle customers.

Now, with all that being said, let's move forward with the basics of marketing and how you can increase your business through marketing.

Marketing vs. Advertising

When most people think of marketing the first thing that pops into their head is an advertisement. This leads many people to believe that marketing and advertising are actually the same things. They aren't.

Here is the definition of marketing according to Merriam-Webster's online dictionary:

Marketing is "the process or technique of promoting, selling, and distributing a product or service."

And here is the definition of advertising according to Merriam-Webster's online dictionary:

Advertising is "the action of calling something to the attention of the public especially by paid announcement."

So you can see that by definition, marketing is much broader than advertising. Advertising is actually a part of marketing. But it's not the only part of marketing. Sure advertising is a major part of marketing, but it isn't even the majority of marketing. So don't ever make the mistake of confusing advertising with marketing. The two terms are not interchangeable. And marketing is much larger than advertising.

Always remember this. Advertising is a big part of marketing but it's far from being the only part. Marketing is so much more. Therefore, in order to be successful with your marketing efforts, you have to concentrate on much more than just advertising.

What is Marketing?

The next logical question to ask is: What is marketing?

You just read the definition of marketing above. And from that definition you can see that marketing is pretty much everything. This is a fact that you need to always remember.

Marketing is everything!

It's everything you think it is and it's everything that you never thought was part of marketing.

For example, one specific way you can improve your business and make more money is by making sure you always answer the phone politely and with a positive tone. Many small business owners overlook this one small tip, and they probably lose a lot of business because of it. Phone calls and the way you deal with people over the phone are a part of marketing.

There are many different people who call you and these people call for many different reasons. These calls come in at all different times and you might be doing absolutely nothing or you might be very busy. No matter what you're doing you need to make sure you answer the phone politely and professionally, and then you want to make sure you sound pleasant and upbeat when you realize it's a potential customer. Because the majority of calls you get are probably potential or current customers.

Just by making sure you have proper phone etiquette you'll ensure that you don't lose any business and that you capture any potential customers who aren't sure they want to hire you. But this is just one part of your business that needs to be looked at as part of marketing.

In fact, everything you do is part of your marketing efforts. Sure, marketing is the mailing you do once a year and marketing might be calling past customers to see if they need your services again. And marketing is putting flyers around the neighborhood and giving away Frisbees with your business name on them. Marketing is all of the direct efforts you make to promote your business.

But marketing is so much more than this too.

Marketing is also the vehicle you drive, it's the way you talk to each of your customers (every word you say), it's the quality of the work you do, and it's even the clothes you wear.

To be more specific, all of these things go into your brand. Branding is a major part of marketing. Many would argue branding is the most important part of any marketing plan. But we'll get into branding in the next chapter. Right now, let's take a look at the importance of a marketing plan and strategy.

Marketing Plan

If you want to accomplish a goal then you need a plan. It doesn't matter how small or large that goal might be; you always need a plan. If you're taking a short trip to the grocery store you need to plan out exactly how you'll get there. If you're planning to climb Mount Everest you need a plan for how you will train and eventually get to the top of that mountain.

So, to be successful with your marketing efforts you need to have a plan. The plan has to be detailed and it has to be written out. Without detail the plan will allow for you to veer off track. If you don't write the plan down then you won't be accountable to it. But if you do write it down then the plan will actually motivate you and will keep you on the right track.

But how do you begin to put together a marketing plan? Well, it all has to start with a message.

Begin with a Message

In order to properly put together a marketing plan you first have to figure out your message. You need to decide on what you want your business to say to people. This message will be laced through everything you do.

The message needs to grab the attention of people and make them want to use your business. The message also has to set you apart from other people.

In order to help you come-up with a message go grab your local phone book. Turn to the yellow pages and look-up whatever business you might be marketing. Now grab a pad of paper and a pen. You're going to sit down and take a look at all your competition.

The key is to see how you're competition is selling their services so that you can come-up with your own unique selling point or unique selling proposition. This is commonly called a USP and it's essential to your marketing message. You need to set yourself apart from your competition. You need to have a USP.

To completely understand what a USP is let's quickly breakdown each letter.

> ➤ The "**U**" stands for unique. This means you set yourself apart from your competition. Not only should you stand apart from your competition, you need to actually stand above your competition. You need to rise above them.

- The "**S**" stands for selling. It convinces people to buy what you're selling. So in this case you are convincing people to buy your businesses product or service.

- The "**P**" stands for position or proposition. Position is just where you place yourself in relation to your competition. You want to place yourself above everyone else. Proposition is trying to sell something to others. In this case, you're trying to sell something that is a cut above everything else.

Now that you we've broken down USP, let's get back to the yellow pages.

When you're ready with the yellow pages and your pad and pen, go to the first advertisement. List all the promises and benefits that are made in the first advertisement. For example, if they promise quick service then list that. If they guarantee their work then list that. Write down every statement that tells something good about the business.

Now go onto the next ad and put a put a mark beside each time one of the benefits or statements you wrote down appears again. If a new one pops up then write that down.

Keep going through each ad and repeating the process. When you've covered all the ads you'll have a list of promises and benefits along with how many times they each appear in all the ads for your industry.

It's more than likely that all the ads are shockingly similar, right? All your competition is saying the same thing. Sure, there are probably great benefits that are being advertised but if they're all the same then how can any one business hope to be successful with their ad? Obviously they can't.

If you want your marketing plan to be successful then you need to stand out from your competition. This means you have to be unique. You need a USP. But how do you get your very own USP? Well, before you actually look at your own business and come-up with a great idea, you should first look at the USPs used by other businesses.

Coming-Up with Your Own USP

A USP doesn't have to be a tagline or a sales slogan but often it is. Obviously your USP won't work if nobody knows about it. So you need to make sure your USP is somehow part of all your marketing efforts.

Some of the most successful USPs include:

> ➤ Dominoe's Pizza promising to deliver your pizza in 30 minutes or the pizza is free.

> ➤ FexEx promising to absolutely deliver a product overnight.

> ➤ The Subway chain positioning itself as a fast food alternative that will help you lose weight.

> ➤ American Express credit cards claiming they are accepted everywhere in the world.

A great USP can be anything about your business that provides a benefit to your customer that other businesses don't. But it doesn't have to always be a benefit.

A great example of this is the McDonald's fast food chain restaurants putting on all their signs, just below the "M" that they have "over one billion served" or whatever the number might be right now. This USP basically claims that McDonalds is a very popular place to eat and therefore it must be great. This actually feeds in to the "herd" mentality that exists in society. People love to follow others, so a person seeing that so many other people have eaten in a restaurant will be more likely to eat at that restaurant.

To begin to come-up with your own USP, it's a great idea to begin to try to figure out each company's USP while looking at advertisements. With every ad you first want to ask yourself if the business has a USP. If they do (and most should) then try to identify how the USP works. Finally, take a few minutes to think about if there's any part of the USP that you can use when you sit down to figure out your own USP. If the business doesn't have a USP then you can try to figure out one for the business (just for your own learning).

Even if you can't take anything directly from another business's USP, you can still learn a lot just by studying other USPs. You can also get in the right mindset so that you can create your own USP.

And when you sit down to create your own USP, you should start with one question. That question is:

> **Why should a person choose my business over any other business?**

Your USP should answer that question.

And it should be that question that is always in the back of your mind while you're coming up with your own USP. Because if you can come-up with a great USP – a great answer to why people should choose your business – then you will get a lot of customers, make a lot of money, and your business will be a success.

That's the importance of a USP. It can and often does make the difference between success and failure.

In order to come-up with your own USP, there are some very specific idea-generating steps you can go through.

But before we get to that, let's take a look at 6 precious facts you might want to think about when creating your own USP. Most of these probably won't come as any surprise to you. But it's good to be reminded of them.

- Customers like honesty.

- Customers will be loyal to a business that they trust.

- Customers like a good job done as fast as possible.

- The more professional you look the more attractive you'll be to the majority of potential customers.

- Customer service should be your number on priority at all times.

- Not all potential customers are equal. Therefore, not all potential customers will react in the same way to a USP.

There you have 6 facts to always keep in mind.

The last one needs a little explaining.

Not all customers are the same. People have different likes and dislikes and people respond to certain things differently. So you need to make sure you're catering your USP to people who would be interested in your service. For example, a USP that might be very effective at attracting teenagers probably wouldn't be effective at attracting the elderly.

In this case, you need to make sure you gear your USP toward people who would want your product or service. While this includes a large number of people and a diverse group of people, you should still keep it in mind. For the most part you want to make sure you cater to people in your area and that you make sure your USP is broad enough so that it's effective on everyone. Make sure your USP won't turnoff an entire segment of homeowners.

Now that these 6 facts are out of the way, let's get into the exact steps you need to take in order to come-up with your own USP.

Step 1: List all your benefits

The first step to coming-up with your own USP is to list all the benefits you offer customers. This would be things like you work fast, you're reliable, etc. Once you have all your benefits down then you want to choose the top 3 benefits.

You'll see that the next step is to be unique. However, try to think of benefits that are unique during this first step as well.

Step 2: Make it Unique

Now you'll take the 3 best benefits you offer and you'll make each one of them unique. The key here is to put a twist on your benefits so that they become unique.

For example, if you clean windows faster than your competition then you will want to put a unique twist on it like you'll clean windows within 48 hours or the windows will be cleaned for free.

Guarantees are actually a great way to make a benefit unique. You can think of a creative guarantee for just about any benefit.

Step 3: Solve A Need

If you can identify a need or a problem that people in your area have then answering that need or problem would be a great USP. This is exactly what Dominos Pizza did with their 30 minute guarantee. They realized that people who ordered pizza were usually in a hurry and didn't want to have to wait to get their pizza. So they guaranteed their pizza would be delivered in 30 minutes or less. The result was a wild success.

Staying with the window cleaning example from above most people who need to have their windows cleaned either don't have the time to do it themselves or they can't physically do it. So, it would stand to reason that they would continue to have that need throughout the year. You could answer that need by promising 50% off for every repeat window cleaning job you get called for.

These are just a couple ideas. You can probably think of your own unique idea that will allow you to create your own effective USP.

Step 4: Be Specific

You need your USP to be very specific. The last thing you want is to create confusion with what you're offering. So make sure you're very specific with all your ideas.

Step 5: Write Down Your USP and Perfect It

Once you've completed the first 4 steps, you're ready to choose a USP for your business. Write it down. Then tweak it until it sounds perfect.

Your USP should be as short as possible but as long as it needs to be. In other words, it should clearly state what you want it to state but there should not even be one extra word in it.

You'll probably want to write down your USP and then wait a day or so before you begin to edit it. Also, allowing a couple other people to look at it and make suggestions is always a good idea.

Once you've got your USP then you need to make sure you can actually live up to it. Don't just use a USP that sounds great but is impossible to live-up to. And make sure your USP will be good for you and your business too.

Sometimes we get so wrapped-up in a USP that's good for the customer that we completely forget about ourselves. For example, "We'll clean your carpets within 24 hours for half the price of our competition or we'll pay you" is a USP that will attract a lot of customers but it will also kill your business. So make sure you keep your own abilities and needs in mind when creating the USP.

Once your USP is all set and ready to go, you should then make sure it's on all your marketing materials. This needs to include your business card, all your advertisements, invoices, postcards, your Website, letterhead, and everything else.

This includes any type of marketing that you might take part in. And remember, everything you do that's related to your business is and should be considered marketing. Your USP should also be part of your elevator speech. (We'll discuss your elevator speech more in Chapter 3.)

Again, just as this book opened with a reminder that you'd better be willing to do a good job before you even start to think about marketing, you'd better be ready to deliver on the promise of your USP before you start using it. Otherwise, you will get the reputation that you don't live-up to your promises. This will kill your business faster than anything else.

To ensure you'll be able to live up to your USP, and to ensure you're able to market your business effectively, you need a plan. And this brings us back to what we started to discuss at the beginning of this chapter, the importance of having a marketing plan and strategy.

Building a Marketing Plan and a Winning Strategy

Obviously what's covered in the rest of this book will greatly aid you in creating your own marketing plan. So don't try to sit down and write your plan right now. You do need to read the rest of this book first. But now is a good time to briefly go over what you need to have in your marketing plan.

You will build your marketing plan around your USP. Every part of your marketing plan should be related to your USP. But obviously your marketing plan has to go much deeper than your USP. Your marketing plan should be very detailed and include what you need to do each and every day and what your goals are and how you'll achieve those goals.

When putting together your marketing plan you need to consider how much money you have to spend (if any) and how you will spend that money.

You also need to think about all the free ways there are to market your business and then plan which ones will work best for you. As with all marketing tactics, you need to keep in mind your target customers. Don't waste your time (or money) doing anything that won't work.

Now, it has to be pointed out that a marketing plan is absolutely essential if you want to be successful. Sadly only about 1% of all private contractors actually make a detailed marketing plan. They don't even realize how much business they're losing without one.

All research points to the fact that businesses that have a marketing plan outperform those who don't have a marketing plan by about 30%. So, if one business is making $40,000 a year without a marketing plan, that business owner could be making as much as $52,000 with a marketing plan, if not more.

A marketing plan is just that important.

But the fact that most businesses don't have a marketing plan is actually a good thing for you. Not only will you benefit from carefully making a marketing plan but you'll also have a major leg-up on your competition. Odds are that most, if not all, of your competition lacks a marketing plan.

Without a plan you won't really know what you're doing at any given time. Most private contractors will throw an ad in the paper here and might put some flyers on a few bulletin boards there. But there is no consistency and no organization to what's happening.

But with a marketing plan, every bit of marketing you do will be part of your plan. Therefore everything will link together and serve as a guide that will lead to your success.

And putting together a marketing plan doesn't have to be complicated either. In fact, you can write the bulk of it in one day. In just a few hours on one day each year, you can pretty much put together a marketing plan for the entire year.

Here is an easy 4 step process you can always follow for writing out your marketing plan:

1.   **Set Your Sales Goals**

The very first step when writing your marketing plan has to be to set your sales goals. How much money do you want to make? How many clients do you want to attract?

Carefully consider these questions. They should be optimistic but not unrealistic. In other words, don't underestimate the amount of money you can make and the number of clients you can attract. But don't set an unrealistic goal either. You want to set a goal that will force you to work hard to achieve it but not cause you to become frustrated because you can't reach it.

If necessary, you might have to re-adjust your goal (higher or lower) depending on how the year is going.

2.   **Review Past Years (or Consult This Book)**

If you already had a year when you made a marketing plan and followed it then making another marketing plan will be very easy. But most likely, right now, you haven't ever made a marketing plan. So for this year you will heavily rely on this book. But in subsequent years you will look back at your previous years and review which marketing tactics worked and which marketing tactics didn't work.

To help with this, you need to make sure that you always review each and every marketing tactic you used. Take the time to write down whether a particular marketing tactic worked and how it can be improved. Include as much detail as possible. Then you can improve on each tactic that worked and you can throw away any tactic that didn't work.

3.   List all Your Ideas and Important Details

The next step is to write down all your ideas. Anything that sounds like a good marketing idea should be written down. If you have past years to look at then you should list all the ideas that worked last year. If not then most of your ideas will come from this book.

You also want to think about how much money you want to spend on marketing. Obviously some of what you can and can't do will be limited to what you can and can't afford to do. When you actually make out your marketing plan make sure you set aside about 20% of the money in your marketing budget for any marketing opportunity that might arise during the year.

4.   Write Out Your Marketing Plan

Now you're ready to take everything you've written down and make it into a plan. Simply take a calendar and begin planning out how you will market your business throughout the year. Be sure to keep in mind the time of year when the demand for your service is at its highest and lowest demand. You will want to market accordingly.

As you list each marketing tactic you want to make sure you include as much detail as possible. You want to include what you will need to do in order to make the promotion happen. For example, if you're going to pass out flyers then you need to include how and when you will create the flyer, get it printed, and then distribute it. You also want to include how much it will cost you in both time and money.

Then you also want to include details such as:

- ➢ When you will start the campaign and end the campaign.
- ➢ Where you will run the campaign.

> ➤ If the promotion will be a one time deal or if it will run multiple times. If so, will it be run the same way?
> ➤ The number of customers you hope to get from the promotion.
> ➤ The amount of money you hope to make from the promotion.
> ➤ The average amount of money you hope to make from each job you get.

The exact details you'd have in your plan will depend on exactly what you're doing and what you want to accomplish.

Every marketing plan has one main goal that you need to achieve. For example, the main goal of your marketing plan might be to produce flyers that you'll distribute to potential customers. However, you will have smaller goals within your plan that will lead to you accomplishing the major goal. The smaller plans would be creating the copy you want on the flyer, creating graphics, getting the flyers printed, and then actually distributing the flyers.

Then under each smaller goal you'll list the steps you need to take in order to accomplish each goal. The details will include each detailed step, when the job will start, how long it will take, and when it needs to be completed. It will also include who will complete the task, any special details about how it will be completed, and how much it will cost to complete the task.

Most marketing plans are written on a spreadsheet. The spreadsheet will have a columns that will be divided for each of the details listed above. So you will have a column for the task, how long the task will take, when the task will begin, when it will end, etc.

Obviously your marketing plan will have to line-up with your budget as well. You can't spend, or plan to spend, money you don't have. But as long as you use a detailed plan, you don't have to.

But there are plenty of low cost or no cost marketing techniques that you can use. Then as your marketing begins to make you money, you can step-up your marketing efforts and start spending more for marketing.

Writing out a marketing plan for the entire year will basically ensure that you won't ever have a down time during the year. It will also help keep you organized throughout the year as you continue to grow your business.

By writing down your marketing plan you will be able to look at it regularly and know that you are on track. Also, a marketing plan that's written down will serve as motivation for you. You can always see what you're supposed to be doing and then make sure you are doing just that.

Your marketing plan for the entire year will be very similar to the written plan you'll have for each individual marketing campaign. However, it will obviously be larger in scope and not nearly as detailed. So you will simply list each campaign you want to run during the year, when the campaign will be, and other major details, but the plan won't get into any specifics.

Let's face it: You are much more interested in your product and making money. You aren't so into the idea of marketing your business. And it's very easy to stop marketing your business when things are going well. However, this will lead to you running out of customers. And this will hurt your business.

To make sure you're always marketing your business and that you will never have a time when you aren't making much money, make sure you write down a detailed marketing plan. And then make sure you follow throughout the year.

Summing Up Chapter One

Now you know the importance of a marketing plan. You also know the basics for how to put together a marketing plan. As you go through this book you will discover the details you want to put into that marketing plan.

Now you also know how to figure out your USP and what to do with it. You should always keep your USP in mind when putting together your marketing plan and you should also make sure your USP is part of all your marketing promotions. Often a USP is part of (or even your entire) slogan.

Now it's time to get back to marketing in general. It's time to talk about a term that is very closely related to much of what was discussed in this chapter. It's time to discuss branding, and that's just what we'll do in Chapter Two. We'll also take a look at elevator speeches – what they are, why you need one, and how to create one.

Chapter Two

Branding and Elevator Speeches

In the last chapter we laid a strong foundation that will allow you to create and grow your business through marketing. In the next chapter we're going to begin to look at some very specific marketing promotions you can use for your own business. Specifically we'll get into how to write great newspaper ads and ads in the yellow pages. This is just one topic we'll cover next.

But before we do that, we need to cover a couple more marketing basics that will help complete the foundation you can build upon.

Branding

It's very tough to pin down one exact definition for branding. Sure, you can look it up online or in a dictionary but it will still be tough to come-up with just one definition. What you need to know is branding is the way a product or even an entire company is presented and the way that people see that product or company.

So branding is the slogan, the colors, trademarks, symbols, and anything else that goes along with the presentation of a product or a company.

Nike is a company that has done an outstanding job with branding. Everyone knows Nike's swoosh symbol. You're also probably familiar with the "Just do It" slogan. Also, for years Nike published a lot of posters with athletes and dark backgrounds. That was part of their branding too. It was dark and a little edgy. It was hip. To add to this brand Nike loves to combine music, cool scenes, and popular athletes.

All the athletes that Nike sponsors are also part of their brand. In fact, sponsors are a major part of branding for any company. That's why it's so important for athletes not to get in trouble. An athlete that gets in trouble is a direct reflection on the sponsoring company. That's bad. But when an athlete does something great, that gives a great boost to the product and/or company.

The 2008 Summer Games showed just how important branding really is, and how branding works. Many of the best swimmers for the United States were sponsored by Nike.

However, a rival brand of swimsuit, Speedo, had invented a swimsuit that allowed a swimmer to swim through the water with little or no resistance. Therefore a swimmer wearing a Speedo suit automatically had an advantage over a swimmer wearing a Nike suit. So Nike made the business decision to allow all of their sponsored swimmers to wear Speedo suits.

The decision by Nike was completely based on branding. Sure, they hurt their brand a little by not having their sponsored swimmers wearing Nike suits while they were in the water during the Olympics. However, by allowing their swimmers to wear Speedo suits, Nike was giving their swimmers every opportunity to win medals at the Olympics. Winning medals at the Olympics would boost the popularity of their athletes and thus increase brand awareness for Nike.

So Nike gave-up a little bit of branding in the short term in order to gain a lot more attention in the future.

So branding is pretty much everything that goes into painting an image of your company and the service you provide. It's your logo, your USP, your slogan, the colors you use on all your promotional materials, and anything else the public sees. Branding is also how you treat your customers.

Just as you're always marketing, you should be aware that most of the time you are also building your brand. So make sure you have a very clear picture for what you want your brand to be and make sure you include branding in your marketing plan.

How to Build Your Brand

When building your brand, the first thing you need to know is that you don't actually perceive your brand, everyone else does. Therefore, you need to build your brand trying to see things through the eyes of other people.

The second thing you need to know is that the best brands tap into people's emotions. Also, as with marketing (remember USP), you want to be unique with your brand. So set yourself apart from your competition with your brand.

To build a brand you'll need to develop it, define your message, and then market it. Once that's done then you'll present your brand visually, verbally, and through your actions.

As we mentioned above, branding is everything that you do as a business. So, it's your logo, your slogan, and the colors you use. But it's also how you treat your customers and how well you do your job.

When you begin to develop your brand you need to come-up with colors you want for your company, you need to develop a logo, and you also need to create a slogan. Then make sure everything in your business is in line with those things. Make sure all your promotional materials (letterhead, business cards, brochures, signage, etc.) has the right logo, the right slogan, and the right colors. Make sure your clothing, the logo on your truck, and every else matches as well.

Once you have everything coordinated then you need to get your brand out there. Obviously, this starts by making sure your promotional materials are aligned. But you can do a lot more to build your brand.

You can get your logo printed on inexpensive merchandise like hats, golf balls, or t-shirts. You can also give away gifts with your printed logo for holidays and special events. Obviously, you should advertise too, and your ads should all be in line with your brand.

Elevator Speech

An elevator speech is a quick speech that you can give that explains what your business (or a product) is all about within about a half minute or so. It's called an elevator speech because you should be able to give the speech in the amount of time it would take to travel in an elevator. It's usually about 150-200 words. But it can be as little as 10 or 15 words. It just has to be effective in communicating what you're all about and attracting any potential customers.

Most likely a lot of people ask you what you do. Many of these people probably have an interest in such a service or know someone who would be interested. If not, most likely the person will at some point run across someone who is interested in your service.

If you have a great elevator speech then you can reel in all of these potential customers. Elevator speeches are especially beneficial in helping people remember you when they (or someone they know) need your service in the future.

You want to take the time to put together a great elevator speech. And you want your elevator speech to be built around your USP.

To create an elevator speech you just have to list all the benefits you offer (remember you made a list earlier when you were figuring out your USP). Then take the greatest benefits and try to work them into an elevator speech. Be sure to concentrate on what's best for customers.

Creating an elevator speech should be very easy for you since you already created a USP. In fact, your elevator speech could simply be your USP. Just make sure it clearly tells people what you do and why you're the best at what you do.

Also make sure your elevator speech isn't too long or boring. It should roll right off your tongue naturally and quickly. And it should have a hook that will pull in potential customers.

For example, your elevator speech might be something like:

"Hi my name is (insert name) and I'm the owner of (insert business name). We specialize in (insert USP)."

Obviously you won't include your name and/or your business name if the person already knows it. And again, make sure you practice your speech enough so that it flows naturally and doesn't sound forced or rehearsed.

Summing Up Chapter 2

Every little thing you do is a reflection on you and your business. Don't ever forget that. Everyday businesses lose customers for reasons they don't even realize. Don't let that happen to you.

Always remember that everything you do is part of your marketing and just about everything is part of the brand you are putting out there for people to judge you and your business.

Always pay attention to your brand. Make sure you have a plan for your brand and that you stick to that plan.

Also make sure you prepare an elevator speech. It should be brief but as effective as possible. Your elevator speech should tie in with your overall marketing plan, your USP, and your brand.

In fact, all of your marketing efforts should be connected and all add up to form a great marketing campaign.

Now, in Chapter 3, we're going to get into marketing techniques. This will include some specific marketing tactics and techniques. It will also include publicity.

Chapter Three

Marketing Methods and Techniques

In the first couple of chapters we took a look at the importance of marketing and having a marketing plan. We also looked at USPs, elevator speeches, and branding. All of this has to be a part of your marketing plan. However, none of it will help you with the specifics for how you'll need to market your business. In this chapter we'll get into specifics.

Obviously a major part of your marketing business will be advertising in newspapers, the yellow pages, and other places around your service area. But you can also market on the Internet and you can also use some unique marketing techniques. These unique ways include free ways to get publicity. We'll get into all of this in this chapter.

But first, let's look out advertising in newspapers.

Advertising in Newspapers

Let's get one thing straight right off the top: Advertising in newspapers is very expensive. And it's not nearly as effective as it once was. Every single day fewer people are reading newspapers. Even fewer are actually looking at the classified ads in newspapers.

However, newspaper ads are still very important for local businesses. Therefore, you need to use this advertising medium. If you know how to place an ad (and you're about to discover how) then you can really provide a huge boost to your business.

Also, what we're about to discuss in this section will apply to advertising in any type of local publication. So if you have a small trade magazine or a local paper that's all classifieds then you'll probably be able to list an ad for a very reasonable price.

Here are 10 strategies you always want to follow when placing newspaper ads:

1.   **Advertise Consistently**

One problem with advertising in papers is that you could be missing 50% or more of potential customers on any given day. They could be away for the day, they might be too busy to read the paper, their dog might've chewed it up, etc. To avoid this problem, place your ad as consistently as possible.

If you're running a larger ad (and they are the most effective) then you'll want to try to run the ad at least once a week for a few weeks. If you are listing your ad in the classifieds section then you will want to make sure you run it just about every single day for a few weeks.

2.   **Think about the Day and the Time of Year**

Different ads for different products and services will work better on certain days and at certain times of the year. The days you run an ad and the time of year you run more ads should all be thought through carefully and made part of your marketing plan.

As you place ads and keep track of their performance you'll be able to discover what days work best and when the best time of the year is to run such ads.

Here is a quick overall review for each day of the week:

Saturday: Many advertisers believe this is a bad day to advertise their business. But this is actually a good day to advertise. First, there is less competition on Saturdays since most businesses stay away from this day. Secondly, many people wake-up on Saturday and think about the things they have to do around the house. If they see your ad they just might call you instead of doing it themselves.

Sunday: The Sunday paper has a lot of readers. But there is a lot of competition too. However, it's a good day to advertise, especially financial and business related businesses.

Monday: A lot of men read the paper on Monday because of the recap on the weekend sports.

Tuesday: This is a good day to advertise for financial businesses and business related businesses.

Wednesday: This day is best for food related and health businesses.

Thursday: This is a pretty good day to advertise. One reason is because people begin to look for weekend events on this day. This includes people looking for garage sales.

Friday: Again, people begin looking forward to the weekend and they start thinking about what they have to do on the weekend. Maybe they want to go to a music festival on Saturday but they also need to clean their carpets. They see your ad and they call you so they can go to the festival and have you clean their carpets for them.

3.   **Size and Position is Everything**

The size of your ad and where your ad is located is as, or perhaps even more, important than what your ad actually says.

First of all, advertisers used to clamor to be on the right hand side of the newspaper. This is because that's the side of the paper people see as they turn from page to page. However, studies show that just as many people read the paper from back to front as read it front to back. Therefore, it doesn't really matter what side of the paper your ad is on.

What is important is that your ad be placed above the fold. In other words, you want your ad to appear on the top half of the paper.

It's also important to try to get your ad listed in the "main news" section of the paper. You also want it to be as close to the front of the section as you can possibly get it.

Finally, it's important that your ad dominate the page it is on. But this doesn't mean that you need to take out a full page ad. In fact, an ad that is more than 50% of a page in width and height is every bit as effective as an ad that is a full page. Usually this means the ad is at least 12 inches high and at least 5 columns wide.

4.   **Color is Best**

Color ads draw more attention and converts (meaning it will turn potential customers into actual paying customers) far better than black and white ads. Colored ads are more expensive but the extra cost is well worth it. Color will help you catch the reader's eye.

If you can't afford to run a full color ad then simply using one color to highlight or accent the ad (with the rest being black and white) is also effective. Just make sure you carefully choose that one color.

5. Don't Let the Paper Design Your Ad for You

If you let the newspaper create your ad for you then it's probably going to look like every other ad that's run in the paper. Remember you want your ad (and your business) to stand apart from your competition. If possible pay to have your ad professionally done by someone who has a lot of experience with designing newspaper ads. The money you'll spend will be well worth it. But whatever you do, don't let the newspaper design your ad.

6. Test Your Ads (And Track Them Too)

Make sure you test all the ads you run in the newspaper. (This is actually something you should do with all your marketing promotions.) You want to see how much your business is helped with each and every ad you place. And you want to track what happens with all your ads too.

One of the best and easiest ways to do this is to include a coupon with the ad. The coupon can be any type of offer. Just make sure it's a good enough offer to encourage people to use it. Then when people do use the coupon you'll know which ad caused them decide to do business with you.

You should test the days of the week you run the ad, where you run the ad in the newspaper, any special offers you make, and the headlines you use. You won't know what works best until you test it and see what resonates best with customers.

7. Make Good Use of Space

You're paying for the space in the newspaper so make sure you use up all the space. Also, make sure you tell the readers everything they need to know about your business so that they can hire you. Tell them who you are, what you do, why they should hire you, and how they can get in touch with you.

8. It's all about the Headline

The headline on your ad will make or break you. The headline has to hook the reader and get the reader to look at the rest of the advertisement. If the headline is good then the ad will be effective (as long as the rest of the ad copy is decent). If the headline is bad then you won't get any business from the ad (regardless of how great the rest of the ad copy might be).

Headlines are so important that there is an entire section on how to write them in a couple pages. This section will teach you how to write killer headlines and it'll also give you examples of great headlines.

9. Make it Newsworthy

It's obvious that people are reading the newspaper for the news. Therefore, try to make your ad related to the news in some way. That's not always the easiest thing to do with some businesses but it's not impossible. For example, during a warm and dry summer you might write something like: "Has the dry summer left your windows dusty and dirty? We'll clean them for you..."

At least try to tie your ad into what's happening in the news. Your ad will convert much better if you can do it effectively.

10. Give it Time to Work

Newspaper ads usually don't work overnight. Many people will cut out an ad and leave it on their refrigerator until they need it. Then when they need what you offer they'll call you.

So don't expect your ad to work right away. And certainly don't feel like your ad was a failure if it doesn't grab a lot of business for you in the first week or so.

This actually brings us right back to the first tip – "Advertise Consistently." You want to keep advertising in order to make it effective. So make sure you give it plenty of time to work before you declare it a failure.

There you have 10 tips to follow in order to place an ad in the newspaper. Again, you have the option of placing a small ad in the classifieds section or placing a larger and more expensive ad somewhere else in the newspaper. Obviously some of the above tips can only be applied to the larger ads.

If you are listing your ad in the classified section then you want to make sure your headline tells readers what service you're offering. Usually people will scan the classifieds looking for a particular type of ad. So make sure your headline catches their eye.

Killer Headlines

Before you even start to write a headline, you need to remind yourself the 3 main functions of a good headline. They are to grab attention, to speak directly to the intended audience, and to deliver a complete message.

An effective headline has to grab the potential customer's attention. If the headline doesn't grab people's attention then that entire piece of marketing will be a complete failure because nobody will ever buy anything from you.

An effective headline also has to be written directly to the intended audience. Obviously you wouldn't use the same words in a headline for teenagers as you would a headline for the elderly. A great way to make sure you're writing to the right audience is to imagine your ideal customer. Then pretend that you are writing directly to just that one person.

Finally, your headline needs to deliver a message. You need to give the prospect (potential customer) a reason to keep reading the rest of what's written. You need a strong message that will get the person to take time to keep reading your copy and to eventually become a customer.

When you actually begin crafting a headline, you want to write it so that the 4 U's are covered. This means your headline should be unique, useful, ultra-specific, and urgent. If your headline is all of these things then it will do its job.

Here's a quick look at exactly what each of the 4 U's means:

> **Unique** – Your headline needs say something that is different. It can't just be the same old thing or your potential customer will ignore it.

> **Useful** – Your headline has to have value to the potential reader. You need to give people a reason to be interested in what you're marketing.

> **Ultra-Specific** – Be as specific as you can with all your headlines. Narrow your message down to just one idea.

> **Urgent** – The key is to get the customer to act right away. So your headline should highlight a benefit that the person will get if they act right away.

There are a couple other keys that you should always remember while you're writing headlines. The first is that you want to tap into the prospect's emotions. (This actually goes along with making the headline useful.) More often than not, people buy based on emotion.

The second key is to always include a major benefit in your headline. This is really easy if you're writing a postcard to announce a 50% off sale. There's your major benefit. However, if you don't have an obvious benefit then you should sit down and brainstorm all the benefits you offer. Then choose the best one and include that in your headline.

Just remember that you want it to be a benefit. In other words, you want it have direct value for the reader. You do NOT want to simply give a feature of the product.

For example, if you were selling windshield wipers, the best feature of the wipers is that they wipe moisture away from a windshield, right? However, the greatest benefit is that they allow the driver to see and drive safely. Understand the difference?

Take the feature of a product or service one step further and write about the benefit it will provide for the potential customer.

Also, whenever possible include "Why" and "How" in your headlines. How conveys that you are about to tell the reader something they didn't know about before (and everyone wants to learn things that will improve their life). Why does basically the same thing. It implies that there is a valuable piece of information (or a product or a service) that's about to be offered. Here are a couple examples:

"Why you'll never have to clean your own windows again."

"Stop cleaning your windows! Here's why..."

Another great idea for headlines is asking a question. This is personal and immediately gets the reader thinking of themselves and their own needs. Here are a couple examples of possible headlines:

"Are you too busy to clean your windows? Now you can spend your time doing the things you love!"

"Are you sick of cleaning your windows? Now, you don't have to do it ever again."

And here is an example of how you can combine both of the above ideas:

"Have you had enough of cleaning your filthy windows? Here's how you can say goodbye to window cleaning forever!"

"Want to know how you can stop cleaning your own windows?"

Feel free to "borrow" these headlines or to put your own unique spin on them. The above headlines are all written by me and I give them to you. Use them as you wish.

In this case, you can use the exact headlines. But for other headlines you see, you can't take them word for word but you certainly can use them for ideas. In fact, professional copywriters do that all the time. They have hundreds (or sometimes thousands) of headlines that they "borrow" ideas from. It's called a swipe file. Every time you see a headline that you like, save it and add it to your own swipe file.

To get you started, here are a few more headlines along with the company that owns the copyright Feel free to "borrow" the general idea...

"Caught soon enough, early tooth decay can actually be repaired by Colgate." - Colgate

"What in the world is wrong with me?" - Prevention Magazine

"Try burning this coupon." - Harshaw Chemical

"Finally, a Caribbean Cruise as good as its brochure." - Norwegian Cruise Line

Advertising in the Yellow Pages

When someone wants/needs anything done the first place they usually go is to the yellow pages. So you want to make sure you have your business in the yellow pages and you also want to make sure your business stands out from the rest of the competition.

Here are 8 strategies to help your business rise above your competition in the yellow pages:

1.   **The Headline is Everything**

Just as you discovered with newspaper ads, the headline is very important. In fact, in the yellow pages it's even more important. You want to stand out from the rest of the businesses that are there. The way to rise above your competition is by writing a great headline for your yellow pages ad.

You might think you need to put your business name or your name in the headline but that's not right. In fact, you want to put your greatest benefit in the headline. Since you already came-up with this with your USP, this should be very easy to do.

The best headline will include what your business is all about and why people should choose it. Just make sure your business name and phone number is obvious in the ad as well.

2.   **Get the Biggest Ad You Can Afford**

When it comes to the yellow pages bigger really is better. You can either have a full page spread or even a 2 page spread. The larger your ad is the more likely you are to attract customers. In fact, making your ad 2 times bigger than most of the other ads will probably net you 3 or 4 times more customers.

Not only is a larger ad easier for potential customers to find but it also makes you look larger and more successful. For many people success means that you're good at what you do.

Finally, in many yellow pages the larger ads are put first. Therefore, a larger ad will allow you to be seen first.

With that being said, you need to be careful not to overextend yourself by spending too much on a huge yellow pages ad. You certainly don't want to spend all or most of your marketing budget on it. Just realize that bigger is better and, if you have the budget, you should spend more money on a larger ad.

3.   **Remember Selling Points and Benefits**

As with any marketing promotion, you need to make sure you include plenty of selling points and benefits. It won't matter how large your ad is or how great your headline might be if the rest of the copy isn't filled with selling points and benefits. You have to tell potential customers why it makes perfect sense for them to hire you or buy from you.

One of the greatest techniques you can use is to include testimonials. People will trust a third party much more than they'll trust an actual business. So always try to include a couple testimonials with every ad you run.

Here are a few other strategies dealing with how to build your ad:

> - Use a font that's easy to read.
> - Include a headshot of yourself. (When you get the picture taken make sure you tell the photographer that the picture will be used for the yellow pages.)
> - Use other photographs too. People love photos. Also include captions under the photos. Just make sure they will look good in the ad.
> - Use all the space you have.
> - Insert a dateline (the year, and the place of your business)in your ad.

> Don't use all capital letters unless it's for a short word such as FREE.

Don't be afraid to be different with your ad. Remember, different will help you stand apart from your competition.

1. Always Include an Offer

You always want to include some type of offer with every ad you place. (Among other things this will help with tracking.) The offer could be 25% off or it could be a free book that you'll send them. Just make sure you make a good call to action (ask them to do something – in this case take advantage of the offer) along with the offer.

2. Test Your Ad First

Your yellow pages ad will run for an entire year. So you want to make sure it's as effective as possible. The only way to make sure it's effective is to test it beforehand.

So, put a similar ad in the newspaper a few months before you run your yellow pages ad and see how it does. Then tweak it and test it again. Keep testing until it's as good as it can be.

This way you'll get great results for the entire year!

3. Research the Best Directory for You and Your Business

In many cities there is more than one directory. If you can afford to put an ad in all of them then that's great and that's what you should do. If not then you need to choose the directory that's best for you.

First of all, there's usually a main book that's put out by the telephone company. For example, AT&T will have a book if they have the telephone monopoly in your area. So this is the book you always want to go with.

If you can afford to advertise in more than one book then you can conduct your own little marketing experiment in order to decide what other directory you should advertise in.

What you do is tear off the covers of all the telephone directories you have in your office. Then when you go on jobs, show your customers each cover and ask them which one they choose the most. The cover that wins is the one you should advertise in.

4.   **Protect Your Ad**

There are 2 parts to this idea.

The first part is protecting your actual ad from competitors who might try to steal your ideas. The second is protecting the look of your ad and what it says when the people at the yellow pages try to get you to change it.

When your competitors see how effective your ad is, they are very likely to try to steal it and make a similar ad. You can protect your ad by simply copyrighting it. You don't need to send away to get it protected either. In fact, your ad is protected under what is called common law copyright. All you have to do is put the following at the bottom of your ad: "© 2017 Your Business Name". That will protect you from anyone stealing your ideas.

When you submit your ad to the Yellow Pages they will probably try to get you to change it. They are used to the ads all looking a certain way. Yours appearing different will almost certainly throw them for a loop. They'll think you don't know what you're doing. But don't listen to them. They don't know your business and almost all of them don't know very much about marketing either. So stick to your own ideas and make them run your ad the way you want it to be run.

5.   **Don't Forget to Track Your Ad**

Again, as with all your marketing promotions, make sure you track your results. That way you can improve on your ad for the next year.

Another great idea for tracking is to simply tell the customer to ask for a different extension when they call. So in one ad you might put "Ask for extension A and in another ad you might put ask for extension B." Then you'll know which ad led the customer to call by the extension they request.

Before we move on, it needs to be mentioned that there are many other less common publications that you can advertise in too. One that is often overlooked is a church directory or bulletin. It's usually relatively cheap to advertise and the credibility you'll earn will make it well worth the money.

When you advertise in a church bulletin people who go to that church will automatically see you as being associated with the church. This will lead many people to like and to trust you from the beginning.

There may be small papers or magazines in your area that can land you similar results. Just keep your eyes and ears open and realize that there's a lot of value to be gotten from these smaller publications. While the circulation might be small, your conversion rate (the number of customers who see your ad and hire you) will be very high.

Direct Mail Marketing

Direct mail marketing is sending out postcards (or any type of mail) to potential customers. Postcards work the best because there's nothing to open so all the mail recipients will automatically see at least part of your message. Postcards are also cheaper to make and cheaper to mail.

It's best if you use your direct mail marketing campaign to announce a special event of some type. (This will be covered more later in this chapter.) You also want to buy a mailing list from one of the many great companies that are out there. A great site for mailing lists is DirectMail.com (www.directmail.com). You can also compile your own list. (In a couple pages you'll see how you can use a box in other businesses to do this. Then near the end of the chapter you'll see how you can build an email list for email marketing.)

You also want to follow these strategies for your direct mail marketing:

> **Create the best headline possible.** As with any type of marketing, the headline needs to capture the reader's attention. Use the advice for creating headlines that was discussed earlier in this chapter, and make sure your headline is as great as it can be.

> **Pick the right image for your postcard.** You should only have 1 image on the non-address side of your postcard. Don't just choose an image because you think it looks cool. Choose an image that fits with your overall brand and/or the goal of your direct mail marketing campaign.

> **Go with one major idea and keep it simple**. You have limited space with the postcard, and you also have limited time with the reader. So, make sure you just focus on one major idea on your postcard and make sure you explain that idea simply so that the reader can understand what you're offering and what they need to do.

> **Use a great call to action.** The "call to action" is what you want the reader to do.

Do you want them to call a number and schedule a free estimate? Do you want them to call and purchase your product over the phone? Do you want them to enter a contest?

Your call to action should be strong. After all, this is the part where you want to get the potential customer to take advantage of your offer. To help your call to action work, make sure the reward you're offering is good enough to get people to act.

The more effort that you require on the part of the potential customer, the greater the reward you need to offer. For example, if you want the reader to go online and fill out a long form then you'd better be offering a great reward for their time and effort.

➢ **Track your results.** With any marketing campaign you want to track your results.

You can see some great examples of direct marketing postcards by going to www.expresscopy.com.

However I do not recommend you use them for your printing needs, they are expensive and their customer service has been very hit or miss. I do however strongly recommend **PSPrint** for all of your business printing needs, I have been using them for years with outstanding results, and their prices and turn around are excellent.

Telemarketing

Telemarketing, of course, is calling people on the phone and trying to sell them a product or a service

When most people hear the word "telemarketing" they cringe. It's horrible, right?

Then why do some people still use telemarketing? Because it works.

And it works best when the telemarketing follows a direct mailing campaign. In fact, telemarketing has been shown to increase the effectiveness of direct mail marketing well over 100%!

Here is how you should follow-up direct mail marketing with telemarketing:

First you want to identify yourself and tell the person why you're calling. Tell them that you recently sent them a postcard and then give them a call to action.

For example, you call and you say, "Hi, this is Joe Smith from XYZ Company. I'm just giving you a quick call to follow-up on a postcard I sent you a few days ago. The postcard was for a 50% discount for XYZ service. The offer will be running out at the end of the month and I wanted to give you a quick call to make sure you don't miss out on this opportunity. So, when is a good time to set an appointment so you can take advantage of XYZ service today and save over $150?"

You can also use telemarketing to contact businesses in your area. To do this you just need a script – what you (or a representative for you) will say on the phone. In the script all you need to do is say who you are, give the reason you're calling, ask to speak with the decision maker at the company, get through the screen to the decision maker, then repeat who you are and why you're calling to the decision maker, and finally give a call to action.

So a basic script would be something like: "Hello this is Joe Smith from XYZ Company. I'm calling to offer a great discount on XYZ. Who in the company handles XYZ purchasing? Rather than just leave my name and number, I'd rather arrange a better time when I can call back so I can speak with him/her. This offer ends in 2 days."

This should get you through the screener to the person who can actually decide to do business with you. Then you can say to that person, "Hi this is Joe Smith from XYZ Company. I'm calling because I'm currently offering a great deal on XYZ. I'd like to personally come in and speak with you about it and give a brief demonstration. Would tomorrow morning or afternoon be best for you?"

Boxes in Businesses

Placing a box in a business can be great for your business. What you do is you run a contest and you have people fill out a brief form with their name, address, and phone number. They drop the form into a box. Then you will have a box full of leads for your business.

There are a number of ways you can get someone to place a box in their business. For example, if you're a window cleaner then you can offer to clean the business's windows for free in exchange for them allowing you to put the box in their place. Or maybe you can work out a 50% discount with a few different businesses. Then you'll have the extra business and you'll be capturing lots of leads.

Once you get all the leads, then you draw one winner for the contest. For everyone else, you get in touch with them and tell them who won the contest but then tell them they won a consolation price and they'll get your service for 50% off or something like that.

How to Tap into What's Hot (or Create Your Own Media)

Now we're going to take a look at 5 ways you can tap into what's hot at any given time in order to really boost your business.

Here are the 5 strategies:

1.   **Networking Works**

Networking is when you meet and create relationships with other people who might be able to help you and your business. On the surface networking is pretty selfish and in the end it is a little selfish. But in order to network successfully you really need to help others out so that they'll be willing to help you out.

For example, you might call a radio station and offer to clean their windows or carpets for free. Or you might call a newspaper and offer to clean every window in their building for free.

Why would you do such a thing? Well, to start a relationship with them. Maybe they'll wind-up hiring you to always clean their windows or maybe they won't. But more importantly, now you've got a foot in the door with powerful sources of media. There's no telling how much this is worth.

Maybe the newspaper highlights a local business every month and now they'll be more inclined to do a profile on you. Maybe one of the DJs at the radio station will mention that you cleaned the windows and that you did a great job. Who knows? But forming relationships with other businesses and people (networking with them) will help you and your business in ways you can't possibly imagine.

Another great place to network is at the local chamber of commerce. If you aren't already a member you need to become one right away. And you should also attend any business events that take place in your area. Usually there are monthly meetings or events for local businesses. (Just make sure you have your elevator speech prepared before you go to such an event.)

There are other organizations you can join too. These will help produce leads (potential customers) for you. LeTip International (www.letip.com) is one organization. BNI (www.bni.com) is another great organization.

Networking is the most powerful marketing tool you can use. So if you have a limited budget, always be on the lookout for networking opportunities. (This will be discussed more in Chapter Four when we look at targeting commercial and residential customers.)

2. Use Holidays and Seasons to Your Advantage

You can tie many of your marketing promotions into holidays and seasonal events that are taking place. At any given time during the year there's almost always something going on.

Here's a quick rundown of just a few of them (in the order that they happen): New Years, Martin Luther King Day, Valentine's Day, Presidents Day, April Fools, Easter, Earth Day, Mothers Day, Memorial Day, Fathers Day, Fourth of July, summer specials, Labor Day, fall, Columbus Day, Halloween, Thanksgiving, Chanukah/Christmas, and New Years.

And this is just a sample of the major holidays. If you look at most calendars you'll see that just about any day has some type of holiday attached to it.

As often as possible, tie into these events and holidays. Offer promotional materials that might go along with a certain time of the year.

For example, on the Fourth of July you might sponsor a float for the local parade. Or maybe you'll pay to have your business logo and phone number printed on red, white, and blue Frisbees. Then you can walk around the parade and handout the Frisbees to kids.

Another example would be running an ad at the beginning of summer (or in the spring) that talks about enjoying the summer sunshine. You could highlight how great it is to have the sunlight streaming into your house. Then go into the importance of having clean windows that actually let the sunshine in. (Can't you hear the radio ad now? That song from the musical *Hair*, "Let the Sunshine In," would be playing in the background.)

3.   Grab onto other Fads

There are lots of other trends and fads you can tap into as well. You can also look at what's making news and create a marketing promotion around that. Even if it doesn't relate to your specific service, you can still tie into it.

For example, for the last few years Global Warming has been a huge issue. Almost everyone wants to do their part. So, you could run an ad that you use products that are completely natural and eco-friendly. You would tie into the movement for everyone to go green. This could be a big promotion around Earth Day.

4.   Always Look for the Latest and the Greatest

Always keep your eyes and ears open for the latest and greatest invention in your business. If a product is created that revolutionizes the way carpets are cleaned then you want to be the first to get it. If you are then you can advertise that you have technology that none of your competitors have.

5.   **Use Movies and Other Forms of Entertainment**

Movies and other forums of entertainment – sporting events, award shows, concerts, etc. – always offer a great marketing opportunity. People are always talking about these things. If you can tap into them then you can really boost your business.

For example, if there is a huge event coming to your town, you could run an ad that mentions the need for everyone to get their home looking as nice as possible for all the people who will be coming into town. Part of that would be getting their windows and or carpets cleaned.

All of the above ideas are great ways for marketing your business. However, with the possible exception of #1, they all cost money.

How to Get Free (or Nearly Free) Publicity

There are many different ways you can market your business. These ways go beyond simply making sure everything you do is making you and your business look good. Almost all types of marketing will cost you money. However, there are many marketing techniques that won't cost you a dime.

You've probably heard the saying: "There's no such thing as bad publicity." Well, this isn't exactly true. In fact, bad publicity can sink a business quicker than anything else. There are more than a few companies – some of them huge companies – that were ruined just because they got bad publicity.

But most of the time publicity is a great thing. And there are a few different ways that you can get publicity that's completely free (or nearly free).

Of course you want to make sure that all the publicity you get is positive publicity. And the publicity you're after is through the media. (Later in this book we'll go over how to write a press release so you can let the media know when you're doing something extraordinary.)

The first type of great publicity is donating to a charity. Obviously this isn't free publicity but the media coverage you get is often worth much more than the amount of money you donate.

For example, you might donate $2,000 to the local fire department so that they can buy some new equipment. The local newspaper and the local television station come out and cover it. So you're on the 6 o'clock news and the 11 o'clock news. You're also in the paper. Not only are people seeing you and your business but they're also seeing what a great person you are. Pretty much everyone who sees this news story will choose you if they need what you are selling. This includes businesses in the area.

Establishing yourself as an expert is a great way to get free publicity. You can write an article on how to properly care for your carpets. Include a couple tips that most people don't know and then see if your local newspaper will run it. If they do then you are an instant expert in your field. And you capitalize on that.

Not only will you get business from people who see your article but you'll also continue to get business because now you can position yourself as that expert who had an article published in a local newspaper.

Another great way to get publicity is to offer creative promotions. The more creative a promotion is the better chance you'll have that the media will cover the promotion. One example would be offering to clean a house's windows free for a year if they win a contest. Of course this isn't very creative. There are certainly more creative contests that you can think of.

But one advantage to running a contest is that you can ask that everyone who enters the contest give their mailing address and email address. This will allow you to build a list of names and addresses so that you can market directly to these people.

Obviously there are more ways to get publicity. However, these are 3 of the best ways.

You can't underestimate the power of publicity. Bad publicity will ruin your business but good publicity can turn you and your business into an overnight success story.

So the first rule of good publicity is to stay away from bad publicity. And then make sure you create your own positive publicity.

Internet Marketing

Since the Internet became available in homes, people have been making money online. The Internet has turned out to be an absolute goldmine for thousands and thousands of people. Obviously you're familiar with the Internet since you got this guide there. So that's a good thing. You already have a leg-up on many small business owners.

However, there are probably a lot of things about the Internet that you don't know. These things can really help your business. And you're about to discover exactly how the Internet can help you succeed.

First of all, if you don't have a Website then you need to get one. It's really quite easy to do. You simply have to get a domain name, get your site hosted, and then have a Website created for you. Most sites that sell domain names also host domains. Two of the biggest sites are Namecheap and HostGator. Both of these sites will allow you to register a domain and then host your domain with them. I prefer to buy my domain name through Namecheap, and get my hosting through HostGator, as it is cheaper.

You want your domain name to be your business name if at all possible. Be sure your domain name is easy to remember and try to make sure it ends with .com.

It's highly recommended that you hire a professional to create your site for you. In fact, you can hire someone to do everything for you – register your domain name, get your domain hosted for you, create your Website, and get it all up and running. If you don't know very much about computers, this is the recommended way to go.

A cheaper alternative to having your own site is to set-up a page on a social networking site. You've probably seen businesses that have Instagram or FaceBook pages. You can easily set your own page up. Even if you don't know much about computers, it won't take you very long to set-up your own page.

Not only will a presence on the Internet help you to look more professional, but it will also land you new customers.

When you set-up your pages you want to make sure you target keyword phrases that will help people find you. So, if you run a window cleaning service in Bedrock then you would want to target the keyword phrase "window cleaning service in Bedrock." You would probably also want to target other keyword phrases like "need my windows cleaned in Bedrock" and "window cleaning services in Bedrock."

What you are doing is making sure the search engines (like Google, Bing and Yahoo) pull up your page when people type those keyword phrases into the search box. So think of anything people might type in to get a window cleaning service and then target those keywords.

You target those keywords by making sure they are sprinkled throughout the text on your page. If you have your own Website then you want to make sure those keyword phrases are in the meta tags (if you don't know what this means then you should probably get your site designed for you and you can just tell your Web developer to do this).

Now, you can also take advantage of many different ways to advertise your business online. This is what Internet Marketing is all about. It's marketing online for the purpose of making money.

You can pay to advertise on the Internet. The huge search engine, Google, has a program that's called "Google Adwords." This allows you to advertise your business for certain keywords. This is just like the keywords you would target for your own site. They should be words that people will use when searching for your service in your area. Because the keywords won't be very popular (since they are specific to your area) this won't set you back an awful lot. However, it will still cost you money.

You can also advertise on other local businesses sites. This will usually cost you money too. But you might be able to find another business in your area that compliments your business. If so, you should try to arrange a deal that will allow them to advertise on your site in exchange for them advertising on your site.

There are a number of free Internet Marketing techniques you can use as well. These include article writing, blogging, social networking pages, and creating videos.

There are article submission sites (for example, ezinearticles.com) where you can submit short articles (about 300 - 500 words) and have them posted on that site so other people can read them.

A blog is short for "web log" and that's just what it is. It's like an online journal. You can sign-up for a free blog at WordPress.com or at Blogger.com. You can even get your blog added as part of your main site.

There are too many social networking sites to list here. However, the most popular ones are FaceBook, Instagram, HubPages, and Twitter. Twitter, which is all the rage right now, allows you to write little blurbs called "tweets" (140 characters or less) about what you're doing or what's on your mind.

Finally, people love to watch videos, and even the most basic videos are watched by others. You can create a basic video and post it to YouTube. You just need to go to YouTube.com and sign-up for an account. Then all you need is a webcam and/or some free video making software.

The more content you have on the Internet, the more likely you are to be found by potential customers. Also, having a presence on the Internet gives you more credibility and it also helps with your overall brand.

You should have 2 main goals with your Internet Marketing: To be found when people are searching for a business such as yours, and to help potential customers with questions or problems. Creating and posting content will help you accomplish both of these goals.

For example, you might have a blog that you update twice a week. On the blog you give helpful tips that are related to your business. Then you might also create 3 basic instructional videos and post them on YouTube. Finally, you might get a Twitter account and tweet a few times a week.

Then you would want to link to all your content from your main site. You'd also want to link to Twitter and your YouTube videos from your blog. This will help people find everything that you have online.

There is a lot that you can learn about Internet Marketing. But now you know the basics so you can either hire someone to set these things up for you or with a little time and effort you can easily set them up yourself.

Before we wrap-up this chapter, there is one more important idea about Internet Marketing that needs to be mentioned. On your site you need to have what is called an "opt-in box." This is box that potential customers can fill out (with their name and email). You can offer them a small gift (a free e-book) or simply some information about your business in exchange for them giving you their information. Once you have their information then you can market to them through email marketing.

Email marketing is just marketing your business through emails. In fact, you can set-up what is called an "auto responder" to send potential customers their free gift when they sign-up. Then you can also set the auto responder to send marketing emails to the person. Once you set it up, the auto responder will completely run on its own. This is on of the best ways of effectively contacting your customers for practically no cost at all.

Summing Up Chapter Three

We covered a lot of important information in this chapter. We started the chapter by discussing advertising in newspapers and the yellow pages. Then we moved on to many other marketing options you can choose to use.

For most marketing practices the key is testing. But for the yellow pages it's even more important. Remember you want to make sure you have your ad exactly right before you run it in the yellow pages since it will be there for an entire year. So make sure you test the ad in newspapers first.

Of course, you won't know if something works unless you track it. There are a few different ways you can track an ad including offering different promotions in each ad and including different extensions that customers will ask for in each ad.

After we discussed the many ways to market your business, we moved onto specific ways to get publicity and/or to market your business. The more creative you get the better off you'll be. However, make sure everything you do fits in with your brand and isn't so far out there that it actually hurts your business.

Chapter Four

Targeting your Marketing Efforts

You might prefer one or the other but most likely your clients are made-up of businesses and homeowners. While many of the marketing techniques you've already discovered in this book will help with both, there are a few tips you need to know that will help you market to each. And there are obvious differences between how you want to approach each one.

In general, when dealing with residential customers you want to remember to be warm. When dealing with commercial customers you can be a little less warm but more professional.

Private homeowners like to hire people they can trust. They also want to like the person that's working for them. In fact, simply being well liked can ensure customer loyalty.

However, with businesses, it's all about the business. They want a good job done. If you don't do the work the way they want then they'll find someone else and they won't think twice about it. Businesses want to be able to trust the people they hire to complete tasks for them and they usually don't want to be bothered beyond that. So businesses will only be concerned with you providing a great service. If you do then you'll be fine and they'll stick with you.

Of all the residential customers the best prospects for your business are people who are wealthy. There are two reasons for this. Number one they have the money to pay for what they want. Number two they live in large homes and typically spend a large amount of money on home services and luxury items.

So, in this chapter we'll take a look at targeting your marketing efforts to residential customers, commercial customers, and affluent customers.

Targeting Commercial Customers

When you begin to target any specific type of customer, the first thing you always have to consider is what those customers want. As we just discussed, businesses are mostly concerned with the job being done well. They also want to make sure you will get the job done when it's supposed to be done without them worrying about it. Other concerns for businesses, depending on the type of business, might be your appearance and the amount of money you charge.

You have to take each business individually and think about what they really want from a business. The first two criteria – doing the job well and getting the job done on time – are givens but other criteria depend on the type of business and the people who run the business. For example, a restaurant would probably want a window cleaner that has a decent appearance and is able to be polite to their patrons. But a small business that is isolated on a dead end street and makes yo-yos might not care how you look at all as long as you get the job done. However, the yo-yo business might consider money to be an issue.

For the most part you shouldn't ever play the money game. Your service is valuable and people will get what they pay for. Ultimately it's up to you though. But if you do offer your service at a discount for some businesses then you'll probably find that those businesses require the most from you.

Now, the best way to attract commercial customers is through networking. You need to make some type of connection with businesses in your area. Business owners are far more likely to hire you if they know who you are.

Probably the best way to network is by joining your local chamber of commerce. Become active with it. Attend the meetings and any functions they might have. You will meet many other business owners in your area. And, with a decent elevator speech, you'll be able to attract customers this way.

You also want to attend any type of business functions that might be put on by other organizations. Get yourself out in public and make connections.

Being involved in charity events is another great way to network. You will automatically be seen in a positive light by other business owners and you'll also have something in common with them from the start – being involved in charity work.

Networking is easily the best way to market to commercial customers. Having a Website will help too. So will word of mouth once you start getting some customers. But to really make inroads with attracting commercial customers, you need to network. Just get to know the people behind the businesses in your area. And let them know what you do and that you can really help them out with your service.

When you decide to target businesses make sure you call ahead and find out the name of the person who is in charge. Also, find out the name of that person's assistant. Then send postcards to each business that are addressed to the right person (make it personal). Then follow-up with a phone call to the administrative assistant and inquire if they're interested in your service. Often the administrative assistant helps make the day to day decisions like hiring people for a service, and the administrative assistant is much easier to get in touch with.

Targeting Residential Customers

Again, the first step to attracting residential customers is to think what they want. They want someone who will do the job well, they want someone who is trustworthy, and they also want to like the person. Let's break down those last 2 criteria because they're very important.

Homeowners first must trust you in order for them to hire you. Trust is always a key to someone making a purchase of any goods or services. But with home services it's even more important.

Why is this?

Well, it's because you will see every room in their home, unless they pull the shades. But most windows don't have shades. So if you wanted to you could see an awful lot while providing a home service. Therefore homeowners want to be able to trust the person who is working at their house.

Homeowners also need to like the person who is providing a service for them. They might not admit this last criteria but it's absolutely true. People do not want someone they don't like coming to their home and performing a service. In fact, people will overlook a couple minor mistakes if they like the person. But most people won't be repeat customers for someone they don't like no matter how well the job was done.

So, the first step to attracting residential customers is to brand yourself as a nice and trustworthy company. Remember that everything you do will be directly related to your business. So always portray the right image.

There are many techniques you can use to market to residential customers. Many of these techniques have already been discussed. But more traditional marketing techniques can be quite effective. This includes sending out postcards about your business, sticking flyers up at all the local grocery stores (and community centers, etc.) dropping your business card off door to door, and sticking flyers under windshield wipers.

Going door to door and sticking flyers under windshield wipers is usually not very effective. In fact, many people see this as more of an annoyance. However, one way to do this type of marketing and have it be extremely successful is to give a free gift.

For example, you could order a thousand small bags and have something like "Here's a free bag of goodies courtesy of (insert your business name here" printed on the bags. Then you could put your contact information on the bag. Inside the bag you could have something that applies to the season.

For example, if summer is coming up you could put a travel sized bottle of sun lotion, a bottle opener, and a magnet. Usually you can also have your business information printed on each free gift.

Giving free gifts will automatically make people like you. Everyone loves free stuff.

Marketing to Affluent Homeowners

Affluent people, people who have money and are looking to spend it for your service, are said to be completely different than people who don't have a lot of expendable income. This is not completely true. However, it is true that you need to market to them differently.

Let's face it: The majority of your residential customers will be people who have money to spend. People who don't have any extra money can't afford to purchase home services or luxury items(at least not very often) and have houses that are small enough to do the house work themselves. So you need to make sure you know how to market effectively to affluent customers.

To begin thinking about marketing to affluent people you have to think about what separates them from people who aren't affluent. The answer, of course, is money. They have it. Others don't.

So money isn't much of a consideration for most of them. Usually affluent people will be willing to pay a large sum of money as long as the job is done the way they want it. And the way they want it might be very specific.

Now, the fact that rich people usually don't care too much about the cost of your service doesn't mean that you should jack-up your prices. It simply means that this should never be used as one of the selling points when marketing to them.

But let's take a closer look at what most affluent people want. Again, they want someone who is reliable and will do good work. In fact, often they have very specific instructions for how they want the job performed. They also want to know that they have a real professional working on and around their home.

So you have to look and act the part. This means you need to be aware of your appearance and you also need to be aware of the appearance of the vehicle you drive.

Many affluent people love to impress their neighbors. You may very well be part of their attempt to impress their neighbors. This means you need to have a nice truck with your business name and logo on the door.

Keeping these things in mind, you'll be able to create the right marketing image. But how do you actually get to market to these people? Well, the methods aren't really any different then for other people.

One great form of publicity is simply being seen working in the neighborhood. People are much more likely to hire you if they see that you've done work for one of their neighbors. With your truck parked out in front of the house, you'll be getting free publicity.

As with businesses, networking is a great way to market to affluent customers. If you can get to know someone in an affluent neighborhood then you can open the door and you'll be able to attract more customers.

A few possible ways to help you network with affluent customers include: helping out with charities, joining a golf club or country club, and belonging to a neighborhood church. Any association you can gain with people will help you tremendously.

But an association with people doesn't have to be through an organization. It can be through people too. For this reason, make sure you give your elevator speech to your doctor the next time you visit him. Give your elevator speech to your accountant too. Give your elevator speech to anyone who is wealthy.

These affluent people might use your service, but more importantly, they might recommend your service to someone in their neighborhood.

It all comes down to opening up the market. If you have one customer from a neighborhood then many other neighbors are very likely to also take advantage of your business. Word of mouth is very powerful and so is having a presence in a specific area.

Summing-Up Chapter Four

In this chapter we discussed targeting your marketing to specific groups of people. We looked at residential customers and commercial customers. We also looked at affluent customers.

You need to consider what people are looking for when they want a service done and then promise that. We went over this and we also looked at some marketing ideas for each group of people.

In the end it all comes down to creating a great brand and then getting the word out about your business. Often the best publicity you can get is achieved through networking.

Chapter Five

Polishing Your Marketing

Now we've reached the final chapter in this guide and we're just about done. We're at the point in the book where we can sum everything up and add tips and tidbits that will make a good idea even better.

But before we build on everything that was already discussed in this book, we need to cover one more topic. That topic is press releases.

Press Releases

Press releases are the way you'll let the media know when you're doing something. If you're offering something that's unique or something special has happened to your business then you can write a press release and send it to all the media in your area.

But you can't just decide to write a press release. You have to have a reason. You need to be announcing something that is newsworthy. Here are a few examples of reasons you might write a press release:

> ➤ Winning an award or being recognized in some other way.
> ➤ Sponsoring a charity event.
> ➤ Partnering with, merging with, or buying another business.
> ➤ Gaining a contract with a large company.

Now, just because you write a press release and send it out doesn't mean that the media will pick it up. But if it's creative or timely then most likely it will get picked up.

Press releases are awesome because they allow you to let get free publicity if one or more media outlets runs a story based on your press release.

A press release needs to be written in a very specific way. Here is the format that must be followed:

Your Letterhead

Contact: (Your Name)   FOR IMMEDIATE RELEASE Phone
Number: (Your Number)
Cell Phone: (Your Cell)
Email: (Your Email Address)

MAIN HEADLINE
Subtitle of the Press Release

Main body (This is what you want to let people know. Use the upside down triangle just like newspaper articles do.)

For more information about the topic or to schedule an interview with (Insert Your Name), call (Insert Name) at (Insert Number).

Where you see all capital letters used, make sure you use all capital letters. Where it's centered on the page, make sure you center it. Be sure to include three number symbols (### - this signifies the end of the copy) just like you see above and make sure you follow all the other formatting.

This is the way a press release is written.

As with everything else, the headline is very important and should include a hook. Just remember you are sending this press release to the media. They aren't interested in a cheap service or a special offer of any kind. They are interested in things that will make a great story and things that others will find interesting and/or entertaining. So make sure your hook is catered toward the media.

For the body of the press release you want to use what is called an upside down triangle. Sometimes it's also referred to as an inverted pyramid. This is the form you want to follow with all your press releases. It's also the way all newspaper articles are structured.

When you use an upside down triangle what you want to do is give all the broad and general information first. Then you want to get more specific. This way the reader gets all the important information first. Then if and when they keep reading they'll be able to get the details.

Now you know the format for a press release but you don't know the exact information to put in it. Remember that your goal isn't to blatantly market your business. Your goal is to get picked up by news outlets. For this reason steer clear of using all capital letters in the body of your press release and stay away from exclamation points. Also, don't write phrases like "call us today" or "discount prices" or "amazing deals."

Instead you want to include quotes from someone from the company (this will probably be you). Try to make the quotes seem like they came from an interview. You should also include the who, what, when, where and why. If possible, throw some statistics in the press release too.

To get a general idea of what to write in a press release, read the newspaper and watch the news. Look for articles or stories about companies and see how they're written. This is how a press release should be written.

Once you have your press release all written, you can then email or fax it to all the local media. You can compile your own list of email addresses and/or phone numbers by calling each media outlet and asking them where you can send press releases.

You can hire a professional to write your press release for you. They'll distribute it for you too. You can count on spending a decent chunk of money on this service. But it's usually worth the cost, especially if you hate writing and aren't any good at it.

If you want a pro to write your press releases for you but you don't have a lot of money then you might be able to work out a discount that includes you doing some work for them in exchange for them writing your press releases.

You can also write your own press release and use the Internet to distribute it. 4 of the press release distribution sites are Marketwire (www.marketwire.com), PRWeb Direct (www.prwebdirect.com), PR Newswire (www.prnewswire.com) and JVV Enterprises, LLC (www.jvventerprise.com).

It's all about Customers

Obviously the success or failure of your business will come down to how many jobs you get. In other words, it will come down to customers. But more specifically, it will come down to how many customers you can attract and how many customers you can turn into repeat and regular customers.

In fact, if most of the customers who hire you decide to keep hiring you then you'll be all set. And if those customers refer their friends and family to you then you'll be an overnight success story.

See why it's so important to make every customer happy? If you really go above and beyond for someone then that person is likely to tell others how great you are and at least some of the people who hear how great you are will decide to hire you too.

Here are 3 tips for great customer service:

1. **Always greet and treat the customer like they are absolutely the most important thing in the world**. They are the most important part of your business world. Don't ever forget that.

2. **Always be able to answer questions in a knowledgeable way.** Make sure you know everything you need to know so that you can be an expert in your field. What might seem like a harmless question from a customer may result in you losing their business if you're unable to answer that question.

3. **Have a set process and policy for handling complaints.** You might need to think about this one for a while. But be consistent with the way you handle complaints, and make sure you always favor the customer.

The bottom line is this: It's much easier (and cheaper) to make money from existing customers then it is to get money from a potential customer. So make sure you retain as many customers as possible.

There are 2 great techniques for retaining customers.

The first is to have an active customer retention program. This means you keep in contact with your customers. You can do this with a newsletter, a postcard, or even a free gift. Maybe send a small gift at Christmas (a calendar magnet with your logo on it is great) and a greeting card sometime in the spring. Another very effective idea is to simply send a "Thank You" note after someone does business with you. Include a coupon for 25% off the next time they use your service. This will do wonders for your business. Just simple gestures like these will really help customers continue to do business with you.

The second great technique for retaining customers, deals with going after customers you might have lost. Keep track of all your customers. If it seems like you've lost a customer then send them a card and a coupon for your services.

It's very simple to complete the first step of retaining customers. Treat them right and give them an incentive to continue to do business with you. However, it's not so easy to keep track of and go after "lost" customers. But it's not rocket science either.

You can buy software that will keep track of customers and help you with customer retention. There are a few different software products. A couple of them can be found at http://www.maritz.com/tlps/Customer-Retention and at http://www.managemore.com/crm/crm-learn.htm.

However, unless you have a large business, you can probably set up your own customer retention program. It can be as simple as putting all your customers into a basic spreadsheet. Plug in all their information and then color code them according to the time when they last purchased from you. Usually the color coding is done for each year but it can be done at 6 month intervals or an even shorter amount of time.

For example, you might decide to highlight all your 2009 customers in blue. Then in 2010 you'll highlight all your customers in yellow. Then in 2011 you might go with pink. Then you can look at your database of names and see which customers you've lost and when they were lost.

Another option would be to include a column for the year on the spreadsheet. Most spreadsheets allow you to search for numbers or words. All you would need to do is update this column every time someone hires you and then just perform a search for a previous year and you'll find customers who've been lost.

The key is to keep your customers happy so they don't become lost customers. But inevitably some people will drop off and these are the people you'll want to try to get back. You can call them or send them a postcard, or you could send them a survey.

Surveys are great because they make people feel like their opinion matters, they allow you to get in touch with lost customers, and they also allow you to find out the areas you need to improve.

Here is an example of a possible survey:

1. Our records indicate that you were a user of XYZ's service in the past but you haven't used XYZ service in over a year. Is this right?
   - O   Yes

O   No

O   I don't know.

2. What is the main reason you stopped using XYZ Company?
   - O   Cost
   - O   Treatment of Customer
   - O   Lack of Satisfaction with Service Provided
   - O   Other
   - O   I don't know.

Please explain your reason:

3. Did you purchase XYZ service from another company?
   - O   Yes
   - O   No
   - O   I don't know.

4. Is there anything XYZ Company could do differently to keep your business? Please explain.

From just those 4 questions you can find out a lot. And the survey is short enough to get a decent response. With every reply you get you can not only try to get each individual customer back but you can also improve your overall business. Remember, the best way to retain customers is to treat them well and provide a great service right from the start.

While you're at it, just as you did with lost customers, you might want to have current customers fill out a survey too. You can even offer a small discount to customers in exchange for them filling out a short survey. Then you can use their feedback for testimonials. You just have to get their permission to use their first name and you can do that by putting a little blurb on the survey that tells them the information they supply may be used for marketing purposes.

Referrals are Priceless

Finally, we already touched on how valuable word of mouth can be. Well you can help rocket that word of mouth by getting referrals from existing customers. So many small business people who offer a service (just like you) fail to even think about referrals. This is a huge mistake. Some marketing studies have shown that the average person is capable of making up to 50 referrals!

To run a successful referral program you just need to need to take care of three easy steps:

1.   You need to do a great job for the customer.
2.   You need to ask the customer to refer you.
3.   You need to reward the customer for referring you to someone else.

That's all there is to it. Just adopting this one change into your business will land you new customers almost immediately.

There are a lot of great referral programs out there. One example is offering $50 to every person who refers a paying customer to you. Or for 5 leads (5 names you can contact) you can give a customer 10% off their own cost.

Again, depending on how large your business is, you might need software to help manage your referral program. But you can usually manage it yourself. If you provide a great service and you treat your customers well then a referral program can be as easy as just creating a form that explains your referral program. Then you can keep track of referrals on a basic spreadsheet.

It's Time to Use What You Discovered

So now you know everything you need to know to effectively market your business.

The most important point you need to remember from this guide is that you must view everything as a marketing opportunity. Absolutely everything!

And then you have to take advantage of each and every opportunity. Take the time to figure out your USP and then build your marketing strategy. Use all the great tips you just read about.

Within just a few months, you'll see how much your business is helped from your marketing efforts. And as you test and then change your marketing plans, your business will only get more successful.

Now, it's time for you to get started. It's time for you to truly market your business and to finally achieve true success.

Resources Section

Marketing Materials Resource

My experience in business has taught me that your image is critical to your success. You will be inside your customer's homes, but before they let you in, you have to show them that you're not some Joe blow passing through town looking for beer money. To that end it is critical that you utilize top quality marketing and business materials in order to ensure a 'good' first impression.

With the above in mind I want to share with you one of my secret weapons, that I use to ensure that all my marketing and promotion materials are of top notch quality without breaking the bank.

The company is PSPrint, and they are in my opinion the best professional online print shop around. They handle all my printing needs for Postcards, Flyers, Door Hangers, Business Cards, Brochures and Promotional Items. I even had them do a few Vinyl banners for me and they turned out great! I can assure you, once you give them a try you won't use anyone else.

Also if you need magnetic signs for your vehicle or yard/street signs for your promotions, then I suggest you check out iPrint, as they have some unbeatable pricing when it comes to these types of signs and even when you add in shipping they are usually cheaper than your local sign shop.